Johnny Appleseed

Johnny Appleseed

by EVA MOORE

Pictures by BEATRICE DARWIN
Cover by RICHARD SCARPER

SCHOLASTIC INC.
New York Toronto London Auckland Sydney

For Johnny's friends everywhere,
especially B. de R.

ISBN 0-590-40297-8

20 19 18 17   7 8 9/9
                          Printed in the U.S.A.   23

Contents

Alone in the Woods

THE road in back of the Chapman house twisted and turned and went right down to the river.

Johnny Chapman came running down the road. He was on his way to his new job — helping Mr. Crawford in the apple orchard. But first he wanted to see his friends.

Johnny ran across the little bridge that went over the river. He ran into the dark woods on the other side. And then he stopped running.

It was quiet in the woods — almost quiet. Johnny could hear the birds singing. He could hear the leaves softly blowing in the wind.

A rabbit ran up to meet Johnny. A squirrel jumped from one big tree to another to get nearer to him. "Here are my friends," thought Johnny, "here in the woods."

The animals of the forest were not afraid of Johnny Chapman. Johnny brought food to them, and he took care of sick or hurt animals he found.

Johnny lived in a little town in Massachusetts. He was only ten years old, but he often spent days and days alone in the woods.

Johnny's step-mother was too busy taking care of her ten other children to look after him. Sometimes she did not even know he was gone.

Johnny liked to be alone in the woods. He liked to play in the river that ran near the woods. He liked to swim in the cool water. But most of all he liked to ride down the river

on a raft he had built from old fallen trees.

Johnny ate the berries that grew wild in the woods. He played with the animals. Sometimes Johnny brought his Bible into the woods with him. He read aloud to the animals, and they would come to him as if they understood the words. At night he lay on the ground and watched the stars until he fell asleep.

And Johnny would talk to the stars and to the animals. He would tell them, "Some day I will be a missionary — a preacher. I will go all around the country telling people about God and the Bible."

But this afternoon Johnny did not have time to play with his friends or read to them from his Bible. He had to hurry. Mr. Crawford, the orchard man, was waiting for him in the apple orchard.

So Johnny waved good-bye to the rabbit and the squirrel and the singing birds. Barefoot, he ran down the path to Mr. Crawford's orchard. Red, ripe apples were hanging from the branches of every tree.

Mr. Crawford liked to tell Johnny about the apple trees.

"Apple trees are strong trees, Johnny," he said as they walked through the orchard. "An apple tree can grow in almost any kind of soil."

"Where did the first apple trees grow?" Johnny asked.

"I don't know, Johnny," said Mr. Crawford. "Apples are one of the oldest fruits ever grown. You can find the word *apple* even in the Bible."

Johnny smiled.

"Yes," Mr. Crawford said. "An apple tree is

a great thing . . . an apple is a great thing. There are so many kinds of apples, Johnny, and so many ways to use them. You can eat apples right off the tree. Or you can make them into apple pies and apple cakes, and apple butter and apple sauce — and apple cider! You can roast apples, bake apples, and boil apples," said Mr. Crawford. He picked an apple from one of the trees and took a bite. The juice rolled down his chin.

"And they're good for you," he said.

Mr. Crawford showed Johnny how to pick an apple off the tree the right way — without breaking the twig.

Soon Johnny was picking one apple after another and putting them into the basket at his feet. Every apple seemed to be waiting just for him.

Johnny Goes Away

THE years passed. Now Johnny was a young man of eighteen. He was very thin and not very tall. But he was very strong.

People all around Johnny were talking about going West. Many were moving into the wilderness — into western Pennsylvania and the territories of Ohio and Indiana. These places seemed very far away to the people living in Massachusetts.

There was plenty of rich land in these territories. There was plenty of room for more farms.

Johnny wanted to see the wilderness for himself. So he said good-bye to his father and his step-mother and all the children. He said good-bye to Mr. Crawford.

"Don't forget all I told you about apples, Johnny," said Mr. Crawford. He gave Johnny some apples to take with him.

And now it was time for Johnny to say good-bye to the woods and all his animal friends.

"I will miss all of you," he said. "I will think of you when I see your brothers in the

far-off lands called the West. Good-bye, little
friends," said Johnny. And he walked away
through the woods.

John Chapman walked away from his home
in Massachusetts. He walked for many, many
miles. He walked for many, many weeks. He
walked through valleys, and over mountains,
and through deep woods.

One day he came to a small settlement just at the beginning of the great Ohio River. This was Fort Pitt.

Johnny liked this settlement. He built a house for himself near the river. He started a farm. But Johnny missed the apple trees he had seen every day in Mr. Crawford's orchard.

So Johnny went to see nearby farmers who owned cider mills. In the mills were cider presses that squeezed apples into juice. The seeds were thrown away.

Johnny gathered these seeds and brought them back to his farm in large linen bags. He washed the seeds and sorted out the good ones from the bad ones. Then, with the very best seeds, he planted an orchard of his own.

The Appleseed Man

DAY by day John Chapman took care of his orchard. He watched his seeds grow into little seedling trees. He watched his seedlings grow into big, strong trees. In about five years, his trees were bearing fruit.

Now there were many people going even farther west than Fort Pitt. These pioneers were moving their families out into the wilderness. They would clear the land and build new homes.

Many pioneers stopped by Johnny's house to rest. Johnny always welcomed them.

If they needed milk, Johnny gave them milk from his own cows. And he gave them butter. He gave them wild honey, too, that he had gathered in the woods.

Sometimes people would ask Johnny, "Why do you give so much honey away? You could sell it for a good price."

"If the bees don't work for money, then why should I?" was Johnny's answer.

Johnny would rather give things away than sell them. When he needed money, he sold some of his seedlings. But if a person could not afford to pay much, Johnny would sell him a tree for just a few pennies.

Most of all, Johnny liked to give apples to the pioneers. He always had some apples on hand — even in seasons when there was no fruit on the trees.

Johnny kept apples in a big cave. A spring in the center of the cave made the earth around the apples cool and wet. The cool, wet earth kept the apples from spoiling.

Johnny tried to tell the pioneers all the ways they could use apples. He was sure they would need apple trees out in the wilderness.

"Apples are Nature's gift to us," said Johnny. "You will need the fruit for food. You will need apples to trade for other things."

Johnny showed the pioneers his own trees. He wanted to give each one of them a little apple tree to take with him. He said, "Take this seedling into the wilderness. Plant it in the ground. Take care of it and watch it grow. Some day it will give you apples like these.

Then you will see how important apples are to you."

The pioneers would take Johnny's honey, but many of them shook their heads at his seedling trees.

"We cannot carry a little tree. We have no room in our wagons. Besides, the tree is too small and weak. The branches will break. It will die before we get to our new land."

Johnny did not want his apple trees to die. He thought of another way to help the pioneers bring apple trees into the West. Soon he was

giving each pioneer a small bag of seeds to take with him and plant near his new home.

But still some shook their heads. "No," said one. "Apple trees will not grow in this land. It is too wild."

"If the land is too wild for apple trees, then it is not a fit place for women and children," said Johnny.

And he had his way. When the pioneers left his house, most of them had a small bag of apple seeds.

The pioneers began to call Johnny "the Appleseed Man." They called his orchard "the wonder of the wilderness."

At night Johnny dreamed of all the apple trees the pioneers were going to plant. He dreamed of acres and acres of orchards blooming in the spring with white blossoms. He dreamed of acres and acres of apples to harvest in the fall.

But Johnny was worried. What if the pioneers forgot to plant the seeds he gave them? His dream would never come true if the pioneers did not plant the seeds.

"What can I do?" he asked his trees. "What can I do?" he asked the stars. The trees waved at him. The stars winked at him. Then the answer came to him.

He decided to go into the wilderness himself. He would go from place to place where apples were needed. "I will show the pioneers how to plant trees," Johnny said.

Johnny had lived in Fort Pitt for twelve years. He had worked hard to make a good farm and a good orchard. Now he was going to leave. He was going to set out for the territory of Ohio. But who would take care of the house he had built? Who would take care of the orchard he had planted?

Johnny knew a poor woman who had children to look after and no place to live. So he gave his house and his orchard and his whole farm to her. The woman was so happy, she cried.

And Johnny was happy too. He knew that he had an important job to do.

Johnny and the Wolf

WHAT was the fastest way to get to Ohio?
Johnny looked at the fast-moving Ohio River.

"The river will take me there," he said.

Johnny put some big leather bags full of
apple seeds into a canoe. He put other things
into another canoe — some food, a cooking pot,
some medicine to cure any sick people or
animals he found in the wilderness, and his
Bible.

Johnny still dreamed of being a missionary
preacher. Now, he thought, he could read to

the pioneers from his Bible. He could tell them that even in the wilderness God was with them.

Johnny tied the two canoes together and started down the Ohio River. It was early spring. The ice had just melted, and the currents in the water were very strong. They pulled and pushed at Johnny's canoes.

But Johnny knew how to handle the terrible currents. As a boy, he had spent many hours riding on his log raft. He remembered the way he steered the raft along the river in Massachusetts.

Johnny paddled his canoes down the Ohio River for many miles. Every night he stopped and tied his canoes to a tree on the bank of the river. He cooked his supper in his cooking pot. Then he found wild berries in the woods to eat, and he made a bed of small twigs and leaves to sleep on.

One night Johnny was awakened by a terrible howl. What could it be? He looked all around him. He saw a dark shadow. It was a wolf. Its foot was caught in a trap.

Quickly Johnny took the wolf's foot out of the trap.

"There now, poor fellow," he said. "I will take care of you."

Johnny tore his shirt to make a bandage for the wolf's foot. He gave the wolf some of the medicine he had brought with him.

Johnny stayed with the wolf until it was well enough to walk.

"Now go back to your home," said Johnny to the wolf.

But the wolf did not run back into the woods. It jumped into one of the canoes. Like a dog who stays with its master, the wolf wanted to stay with Johnny.

Away they went together in the canoes — the wild wolf and the Appleseed Man.

Marietta, Ohio

AFTER many weeks, Johnny reached a settlement in the state of Ohio. When he stopped his canoes, many people came to see this strange-looking man.

Johnny's clothes hung like rags on his thin body. He was barefoot. He had put his cooking pot on his head and was wearing it like a hat.

"What village is this?" Johnny asked the pioneers.

"This is Marietta, Ohio," they said. "Where do you come from?"

"I have come down the Ohio River," Johnny said. "I have some trees for you." He held up a leather bag.

"What's that?" the people asked.

"Apple seeds," Johnny said. "We will plant apple trees all over this wilderness."

Some of the people laughed. "There are many more important things to do," they told Johnny. But Johnny paid no attention.

"Are there orchards here now?" he asked.

"Most of us don't have any time to plant orchards," someone said. "We have homes to build and crops to grow. But there is an apple tree growing in Doctor True's yard."

Johnny hurried to see Doctor True. The tree was there all right. It was full of pink and white blossoms that filled the air with a wonderful smell. For a long time Johnny could only look. And then he said, "The time will come when there will be many trees like this one blooming in these settlements."

Doctor True understood Johnny's dream. He didn't laugh. He wanted to help.

And there were others who wanted to help Johnny, too. A man named Commandant Whipple, of the United States Navy, gave Johnny a plot of land.

"Plant your orchard here," he told Johnny.

Commandant Whipple let men out of the Navy jail to help Johnny plant the seeds. When the little trees started to grow, the men would come back to help him take care of the orchard.

Johnny worked very hard. When the orchard was all planted, he built a fence around it so that no stray animals could get in and dig up the seeds.

But just as Johnny's orchard was beginning to grow, a terrible disease — typhoid fever — struck the people of Marietta. It took many lives.

John Chapman fell ill with the fever. He became very weak. Everyone thought he was going to die. Doctor True worked hard to keep him alive. Little by little, the Appleseed Man grew stronger.

Winter was coming, and Doctor True begged Johnny to stay with him until the cold weather was over.

"Stay here until you are completely well," said Doctor True. So Johnny lived in the doctor's house all winter and helped him take care of other people who were sick.

When spring came, Johnny was ready to leave Marietta. He knew that his friends would look after his orchard. And he wanted to find new places to plant new orchards.

He took his Bible with him and put the tin cooking pot on his head. He promised Doctor True he would come back some day.

Johnny Gets a Nickname

ALL through the wilderness of Ohio, Johnny met pioneers building their homes.

Sometimes he met the same pioneers who had stopped at his farm in Fort Pitt. He asked them if they had planted the apple seeds he had given them.

Most of the men had been too busy. But sometimes Johnny would see a small apple tree growing near one of the log cabins, and he would be glad.

Johnny went deep into the wilderness. He planted his apple seeds. When the pioneers came to clear the land for homes, they found orchards of little trees already growing.

And Johnny was there, taking care of the trees, ready to sell them or give them to the pioneers.

Although Johnny looked very strange to the pioneers, they soon found that he was kind and good.

"What if Johnny is different," they said. "He is always ready to help."

Johnny helped the men build their log cabins. He helped the women wash clothes and make candles. When people were sick, he did what he could to make them well.

The pioneers liked Johnny. They liked him so much, they gave him a nickname. They called him "Johnny Appleseed."

And they began to talk about this man — this strange man who walked through the woods without a gun. Stories about Johnny Appleseed traveled faster than Johnny himself.

One pioneer said that he saw Johnny playing with bear cubs in the woods, and the mother bear just stood by and watched.

Another pioneer said that when a rattlesnake bit Johnny, Johnny did not want anyone to kill it.

"The snake didn't mean it," Johnny Appleseed said. "He didn't know what he was doing."

That autumn Johnny Appleseed went back to Fort Pitt and the cider mills. He came West again with enough seeds to plant many new orchards wherever they were needed.

Johnny and the Indians

As Johnny walked in the wilderness, many eyes looked at him from behind trees. The Indians were watching him. They saw Johnny planting seeds in the earth. They saw deer eat from his hand. They saw birds perch on his shoulder. They saw that he did not carry a gun like other white men.

The Indians were a great danger to the pioneers. They hated the white men. The white men took the Indians' land and spoiled their hunting grounds.

The pioneers hated the Indians. The Indians sometimes made sudden attacks on helpless pioneer families. There were many battles. Men and women and children on both sides were killed.

But the Indians would never harm Johnny Appleseed. They thought he had special magic powers — like their own medicine men.

One day some Indians stopped Johnny on his way through the woods. They said "Come." Johnny followed them to their village. There the Indians gave Johnny presents of beads and fur skins. They put a feather headdress on his head, and they called him "brother." They wanted Johnny to live with them in the village.

At night, in the light of the campfire, Johnny thanked the Indians for bringing him into their tribe. He told them he would always be their brother. But, he said, he could not stay in their village. He had important work to do out in the wilderness.

Johnny tried to keep peace between his Indian brothers and the pioneers. He was able to stop many battles just by talking to the Indians and then talking to the pioneers.

But one day Johnny heard that an Indian tribe was going to attack a small fort in Mansfield, Ohio. There was no time to talk now. And the fort was too small to protect itself from a big attack.

Johnny didn't want to see the pioneers and the Indians fighting. He had a plan.

When it was dark, Johnny ran through the wilderness. He knew the Indians would not stop him. He ran thirty miles in five hours. He ran to the fort in Mount Vernon, Ohio, where there were many soldiers. He told them that the Indians were going to attack the fort in Mansfield. He asked them to come with him to protect the fort.

By dawn, the soldiers were in Mansfield. The Indians who were going to attack saw them, and they went back to their village. There was no battle.

Johnny Appleseed had saved the town. He had saved the Indians, too.

More Stories
About Johnny Appleseed

JOHNNY Appleseed became a welcome sight in the pioneer settlements. He was always invited to stay in one of the pioneer's log cabins. Sitting by the fire, he would read to the family from his old and worn Bible.

Children loved Johnny Appleseed. Wherever he went, children followed him. They begged him to tell them stories. And Johnny loved the children. He liked to tell them stories. And he always had presents of ribbons or calico cloth for the girls.

For forty years Johnny traveled through the wilderness. He planted orchards, and he helped other pioneers plant orchards of their own. Johnny always came back to each of the orchards he planted to look after his trees.

As the years passed, more stories about Johnny were told in the pioneer settlements.

Everyone knew that Johnny walked barefoot summer or winter. The pioneers liked to tell the story of how someone had once given Johnny a pair of shoes to wear. It was winter, and the snow was deep on the ground. Johnny put the shoes on and walked away. The next day the man who gave him the shoes saw him again — barefoot.

"Where are your shoes?" the man asked him.

Johnny told him he had left the shoes with a poor family he met that day. "It looked like

40

they needed a good pair of shoes," Johnny said.

Everyone knew that Johnny Appleseed was kind to all the animals of the wilderness. They liked to tell the story of how Johnny had found a hollow log to sleep in one winter night.

He cleared away the snow at one end of the log and built a fire to keep himself warm. Then he heard a terrible sound from inside the log. He looked — and there was a mother bear and her cub. They were using the log for their bed, too. And they were afraid of Johnny's fire. So Johnny put his fire out. He slept all night in the snow.

Good-bye to the Appleseed Man

JOHNNY Appleseed was getting older. His strong, thin body slowly became weaker and weaker. Now he had to borrow horses to get from orchard to orchard.

Riding along on his horse, Johnny could see how much the country had changed since he was a young man. Villages were growing bigger and bigger. All over the countryside apple orchards were growing.

Johnny Appleseed had made his dream come true.

When Johnny Appleseed was seventy-one

years old, his orchard-planting days were over. Johnny was too old and tired to work in his orchards. But he still liked to visit them, just to make sure someone was taking care of his trees.

In 1844, Johnny went to live with a friend named William Worth and his family in Fort Wayne, Indiana. He spent a happy year with them.

Then one day Johnny heard that there was trouble in one of his orchards twenty-five miles away. Wild cattle had broken through

a fence and were stamping down some young trees. He had to do something.

So Johnny walked all the way to the orchard, and he drove the cattle away. Then he fixed the fence.

This was a lot of work for an old man. It was too much work for Johnny Appleseed.

When he got home, Johnny felt very tired. The family put him to bed.

But Johnny wanted to be outdoors. So they moved his bed outside and put it under the apple tree he had planted in the back yard years ago. It was almost spring, and the apple blossoms were just beginning to show on the tree. Johnny rested under the apple tree all afternoon.

When the sun went down in the sky that night, Johnny Appleseed was dead.

Everyone was sad to hear that the Appleseed Man was dead.

They were grateful for all Johnny Appleseed had done for them.

And they never forgot him. Every spring when the apple trees began to bloom, people remembered Johnny Appleseed. And they remembered him when the trees grew heavy with fruit in the fall.

The apple trees Johnny had planted were valuable. Apples became an important crop, and the beauty of the trees made everyone happy.

But most important, the people had come to love Johnny Appleseed as their friend.

They liked to tell their children about Johnny Appleseed. And when these children grew up, they told their children and their grandchildren.

Today we still tell stories about the man who walked through the wilderness planting trees ... the man called Johnny Appleseed.

Dear Girls and Boys,

Johnny Appleseed was a real person. His real name was John Chapman.

He was born in Leominster, Massachusetts, in 1775 — the year the American Revolutionary War began. He died in Indiana in 1845 — about twenty years before Abraham Lincoln became President.

The pioneers loved Johnny, and they liked to talk about him. They talked about his strange ways and his strange clothes. They told wonderful stories about Johnny Appleseed — stories they thought could have happened because Johnny was such a wonderful person.

Now, when we try to write a biography about Johnny Appleseed, it is hard to tell what stories happened *really* and what ones happened *maybe*.

Everybody has his own favorite stories about Johnny Appleseed. Many people like to think that every apple tree they see was planted by Johnny Appleseed.

Some people say that Johnny planted trees all over the country. Some people say he planted trees only in Ohio and Indiana.

Some people say that Johnny Appleseed played a fiddle and made up poems.

It doesn't matter if all the stories people tell really happened or not. The important thing is that Johnny Appleseed did live — and that he cared.

He cared about apple trees and he cared about animals and he cared about people. To Johnny, every living thing was something to care about. That is why people loved him. And it is the reason we still remember him today.

Eva Moore